THE HISTORY AND MYSTERY OF

TUCSON, ARIZONA

KEN HUDNALL AND SHARON HUDNALL
OMEGA PRESS
EL PASO, TEXAS

THE HISTORY ANFD MYSTERY OF TUCSON, ARIZONA
COPYRIGHT © 2017 KEN HUDNALL

All rights reserved. No part of this book may be reproduced or transmitted in any form or by any means, graphic, electronic, or mechanical, including photocopying, recording, taping or by any information storage or retrieval system, without the permission in writing from the publisher.

OMEGA PRESS

An imprint of Omega Communications Group, Inc.

For information contact:
Omega Press
5823 N. Mesa, #839
El Paso, Texas 79912
Or http://www.kenhudnall.com
FIRST EDITION
Printed in the United States of America

OTHER WORKS BY THE SAME AUTHOR FROM OMEGA PRESS

MANHATTAN CONSPIRACY SERIES
Blood on the Apple
Capitol Crimes
Angel of Death
Confrontation

THE OCCULT CONNECTION
UFOs, Secret Societies and Ancient Gods
The Hidden Race
Flying Saucers
UFOs and the Supernatural
UFOs and Secret Societies
UFOs and Ancient Gods
Evidence of Alien Contact
Sensual Alien Encounters
Secrets of Dulce
Intervention

SHADOW WARS
Shadow Rulers
Underground America

DARKNESS
When Darkness Falls
Fear The Darkness

SPIRITS OF THE BORDER
(with Connie Wang)
The History and Mystery of El Paso Del Norte
The History and Mystery of Fort Bliss, Texas

(with Sharon Hudnall)

The History and Mystery of the Rio Grande
The history and Mystery of New Mexico
The History and Mystery of the Lone Star State
The History and Mystery of Arizona
The History and Mystery of Tombstone, AZ
The History and Mystery of Colorado
Echoes of the Past
El Paso: A City of Secrets
Tales From The Nightshift
The History and Mystery of Sin City
The History and Mystery of Concordia
Military Ghosts
Restless Spirits
School Spirits
The History and Mystery of San Elizario, Texas
The Ghosts of Albuquerque, New Mexico
Haunted Hotels
Haunted Hotels in Arizona and Colorado

THE ESTATE SALE MURDERS
Dead Man's Diary

OTHER WORKS

Northwood Conspiracy

No Safe Haven; Homeland Insecurity

Where No Car Has Gone Before

Seventy Years and No Losses:

The History of the Sun Bowl

How Not To Get Published

Vampires, Werewolves and Things
That Go Bump In The Night

Even Paranoids Have Enemies

Criminal Law for Laymen

Understanding Business Law

Language of the Law

Border Escapades of Billy the Kid

PUBLISHED BY PAJA BOOKS
The Occult Connection: Unidentified Flying Objects

DEDICATION
As with all of my books, I could not have completed this book if not for the support and assistance of my lovely wife, Sharon.

TABLE OF CONTENTS

HISTORY OF TUCSON	11
LOST TREASURE AT THE UNIVERSITY OF ARIZONA	14
CENTENNIAL HALL	24
MARICOPA RESIDENT HALL	30
OLD MAIN	32
MARRONEY THEATER	36
ENGLISH BUILDING	38
MODERN LANGUAGE BUILDING	39
BEAR DOWN GYM	47
ARIZONA STATE MUSEUM SOUTH	54
COLOSSAL CAVE	59
APACHE JUNCTION SEWERS	61
BONILLA'S ELEMENTARY SCHOOL	62
CATALINA HIGH SCHOOL	63

KINO COMMUNITY HOSPITAL	**64**
LI'L ABNER STEAKHOUSE	**66**
LUZ ACADEMY OF TUCSON	**68**
TUCSON MEDICAL CENTER EDUCATION BUILDING	**69**
BLOOM ELEMENTARY	**70**
COLLIER ELEMENTARY SCHOOL	**71**
DAVIS BILINGUAL SCHOOL	**72**
DESERT VIEW HIGH SCHOOL	**73**
DESERT VIEW RANCH	**74**
EVERGREEN CEMETERY	**74**
FOX THEATER	**76**
FRED G. ACOSTA JOB CORPS CENTER	**79**
GARCIA'S RESTAURANT	**81**
FRANCIS OWEN HOLAWAY ELEMENTARY SCHOOL	**85**
HOOTERS RESTAURANT, GOTHAM AND THE NEW WEST NIGHTCLUB	**86**

HOTEL CONGRESS	88
OLD JAIL	92
OLD TUCSON STUDIOS	92
PIONEER INTERNATIONAL HOTEL	99
RADISSON HOTEL	104
SABINO CANYON	105
SAM LEVITZ FURNITURE STORE	106
MAGMA COPPER MINE	107
SAN XAVIER DEL BAC MISSION	109
ST. MARY'S HOSPITAL	112
TUCSON HIGH MAGNET SCHOOL	114
TUCSON MEDICAL CENTER	115
VAIL HIGH SCHOOL	117
VELASCO PUEBLO 1188	
BANK OF AMERICA	120
DAVIS MONTHAN AIR FORCE BASE	121

SANTA RITA HOTEL	123
BARRIO HISTORICO HOUSE	125
CHARLES O. BROWN HOUSE	125
EL TIRADITO	126
OFFICE BUILDING OF ATTORNEY LOUIS W. BARASSI	126
FORT LOWELL PARK	127
22ND STREET ANTIQUE MALL	127
GRANT ROAD GHOST	128
INDEX	129

HISTORY OF TUCSON

In 1821 Mexico gained independence from Spain. The Mexican Occidente state borders extended further north to include the town of Tucsón. In 1853 the United States acquired from Mexico, in the Gadsden Purchase, a strip of land that included Tucson that would later be used to construct a transcontinental railroad along a deep southern route by the Southern Pacific Railroad.

Before the Capture of Tucson (1846) a Mormon Battalion marched across southern Arizona along the San Pedro River, north of Tucson, there the Mormon soldiers fought the humorously named Battle of the Bulls. The Mormon soldiers encountered wild cattle along the banks of the San Pedro River where several bulls charged their column, tipping over wagons and killing mules and injuring two soldiers. The soldiers shot and killed a number of the wild cattle. The soldiers sarcastically named the encounter the "Battle of the Bulls." On December 16, 1846, they marched into Tucson. The smaller Mexican garrison of Fort Tucson, quickly fled without conflict. A brief occupation ensued and then the Mormons continued their march to the Pacific.

In July 1861, after the civil war began, a force of Texan cavalry and Arizonan militia under Lt. Colonel John Baylor conquered the southern New Mexico territory, including Mesilla and Tucson. On August 1, 1861, and the victorious Baylor proclaimed the existence of a Confederate Arizona Territory, which comprised the area defined in the Tucson convention the previous year, with Tucson as its capital. He appointed himself permanent governor.

The proposal to organize the territory was passed by the Confederate Congress in early 1862 and proclaimed by President Jefferson Davis on February 14, 1862. Efforts by the Confederacy to secure control of the region led to the New Mexico Campaign. Later in 1862, Baylor was ousted as governor of the territory by Davis, and the Confederate loss at the Battle of Glorietta Pass forced their retreat. The following month, a small Confederate picket force defeated a Union cavalry patrol north of Tucson at the Battle of Picacho Pass. Despite the Union retreat, Tucson eventually was captured by the California Column.

Tucson, and all of Arizona, remained part of the New Mexico Territory until February 24, 1863, when the Arizona Organic Act passed the Senate forming the Arizona Territory. In 1867, the territorial capital was moved to Tucson from Prescott, where it remained until 1877. In 1885, the University of Arizona was founded in Tucson – it was situated in the countryside, outside the city limits of the time.

During the territorial and early statehood periods, Tucson was Arizona's largest city and commercial and railroad center, while Phoenix was the seat of state government (beginning in 1889) and agriculture. Between 1910 and 1920, Phoenix surpassed Tucson in population and has continued to outpace Tucson in growth. However, both Tucson and Phoenix have experienced among the highest growth rates in the United States.

LOST TREASURE AT THE UNIVERSITY OF ARIZONA

Figure 1: Old Main in the 1890s

If you know where to look there is more treasure to be found on the campus of the University of Arizona than just a great education.

It was in the late fall of 1893 after the weather was just starting to cool in Tucson when the imminent Dr. Ambrose L. Horn arrived at the Territorial University of Arizona in a large cloud of dust kicked up by the Tucson Livery Service's wagon with its team of mules in which the professor was riding in.

The newly elected President Grover Cleveland had just appointed Louis Cameron Hunt, a civil war veteran, as the 11th Territory of Arizona Governor, 15 year old boys could walk into any of the Congress Street Saloons for a drink, the Kingdom of Hawaii had been overthrown by a group of wealthy United States Businessmen secretly working for the government, the Apache & Yavapai Wars had since ended with the 'hostiles' being relocated to reservations or other relocations individually into various cities all around the United States.

The able doctor's long series of traveling on wood burning steam powered locomotives and on stage coach rides from back east had conferred at least some no-nonsense Out West Wisdom into his entire thinking processes. He now knew some of the ways that The West really was.

Tying his fine silk cloth handkerchief around his mouth and nose to filter the dusty blowing desert sand, the doctor jumped out of the back of the horse drawn wagon onto the bare packed Territorial University of Arizona desert sand in front of what was then known as The Arizona Territorial College of Mines in Tucson (now known as Old Main).

Dr. Horn was known in some of the upper circles of the U.S. medical profession of the later 1800's as an unusually exceptionally gifted surgeon, and medical instructor.

After a short period of standing out in the warm sun on the dusty dirt entrance road the doctor was quickly shown to his new home on the mostly desert and cactus filled campus except for the main building located with just a very few sheds and small outbuildings around nearby.

The 1873 stock market crash had lasted until 1878, then not so many years later from 1892 to 1893 in the United States the public experienced first a rampant financial panic, then a stifling depression, finally followed by then an almost complete economic meltdown including a stock market crash and a run on the banks which left many people suddenly penniless. Many banks would suddenly quickly escort their depositors outside, closed their doors, and never opened again while their management suddenly and quietly left town during the night as the population slept.

The good doctor had lost a part of his savings but was not at all in the dire straits of many of the people of the era, many of whom had committed suicide or merely quietly disappeared at night never to be seen again while their families were sleeping rather than face their family and business associates with the reality of bankruptcy.

Doctor Horn's recent employment at the University of Arizona was proving to revitalize his means considerably and rather quickly. But, the doctor's memories of the financial crashes, bank failures, and public panics he had experienced left the professor with a very leery feeling of banks and the ones in Tucson were no exception.

Night janitors along with night owl predisposed students on campus noted observing what they thought was Dr. Horn on various nightly occasions digging in and around what was then the many cactus gardens located all around the dark shadowy unlit 20-acre desert grounds of the college.

Given the already well known eccentricity of both professors and doctors in the latter 1800's era the rumors and matter of the doctor's nocturnal activities quickly passed through the idle gossip phase and were in time almost forgotten just about as quickly.

Then one late stormy night in 1894 as the wind howled through the desert, two members of the football team (both were also members of the same fraternity) were walking around campus after drinking some Red Eye Whiskey they had purchased at the Bucket of Blood Saloon down along the Congress Street area.

Tucson's Red Eye Whiskey in the 1800's often arrived in Tucson in large wooded barrels as a cheaper and always clear grain alcohol liquid. To make it look like the dark expensive whiskey variety, the saloon owners would drop a couple handfuls of rusty nails in the barrels to darken the color of the clear liquid and within a few hours that would give it the very characteristic dark amber whiskey look of expensive whiskey from the East Coast.

On the walk back to the college the two football players' eyes caught the dark shadowy shape of a man off in the distance seemingly bent over near the middle of what is now the University of Arizona's Mall area, which at that time was a very large and well-kept cactus garden.

As the two students got closer they could just make out the figure way out in the distance in front of them.

It was unmistakably that of the esteemed Dr. Ambrose L. Horn crouched over looking down at the ground and tamping down some earth with a small hand trowel such as was used by the school's gardeners.

With the whiskey on their breaths, and not wanting to suffer demerits to their records the two fraternity brothers quickly and very wisely veered off and quietly slipped away into the night unnoticed.

Three days later the two students unable to stand it any longer, and waiting on a moon lit night both then returned to the spot where they had observed the professor mysteriously crouching under the cover of the deserts darkness.

The ground was still reasonably soft, but when it did not yield, one of the boys pulled out a small pocket knife and soon found buried about 12 inches down in the desert soil a small leather pouch with a thin lead liner inside.

Upon opening it up, even in the deserts darkness they could still both see that unmistakable gleaming shine before their eyes.

To their amazement it was GOLD!

And, it was in the form of the $20, $10, and $5 dollar gold pieces struck by the United States Mint.

Quickly getting back to their fraternity buddies the two excitingly woke up the rest of them with the very strange and bizarre news of their find. Quickly they all quickly began devising their plans to secretly search for more of the Professor's hidden hoards of gold coins.

However, what none of the boys realized was that the mysterious Dr. Horn had indeed witnessed the two young football players dig up and abscond with the leather pouch that he had so carefully buried that night under the cover of darkness.

And also what none of the fraternity members could not begin to possibly imagine was the diabolical surprise that the good Dr. Horn was now planning for all of them.

The very clever doctor bided his time until the week of the annual Tucson Cotillion Dance that was one of the most very highly popular events of the 1800's held every year in downtown Tucson at the Ebber's Building to introduce the Tucson Communities eligible girls from all the most socially elite and wealthy families in the area to the very best and brightest of young men from the same social strata then attending the University of Arizona.

As part of the era's requirements for the male college students to attend such a prominent social event it was also required that one of the college's own doctors perform a simple health exam.

Dr. Horn carefully made sure that he would be the schools doctor to perform the exams on the young men. The morning of the exam came with all the most athletic and brightest students of the school soon showing up along with the Fraternity Brothers and each waited to be seen by the doctor.

One local young man patiently sitting in the chair was 'Edward' who was not a student, but the son of a prominent Tucson Businessman, and a patient of Dr. Horn being treated for Dipathentic Laryngitis and had been told to come in that day for his follow up checkup.

Unknowingly, Edward quickly infected all the fraternity brothers with the highly infectious disease that caused those with it to experience laryngitis (the inability to speak), inability to gain an erection, a slight fever, along with vomiting and diarrhea.

Subsequently, the small handful of fraternity members who did attempt to attend the dance despite their mysterious illnesses only lasted minutes before bolting out the exit doors of the building with dark brown stains suddenly appearing down the legs and on the seats of their white formal pants right down to their socks and shoes.

Soon, after each payday, the Professor was once again burying his pouches of gold and silver coins all around the campus under the cover of night due to his total and complete distrust of the banks.

Dr. Ambrose L. Horn died suddenly one afternoon of heart failure while teaching a medical class, and although the face of the University of Arizona campus has changed many, many times over the years since then, only a very few of his money pouches have ever been found.

The ones found are usually during the results of construction excavations or other projects, with the last being in August of 2010.

All of the remaining pouches of now very highly valuable gold and silver coins are presumed to be still scattered all over what is now the University of Arizona campus in Tucson, Arizona.

Recently, a prominent coin dealer on Oracle Road mused, "Considering at various times over the years since that time, the U.S. Governments massive melting down of gold & silver coins, and later in the 1930's the federal governments outright making the possession of gold coins by citizens illegal in the United States, and then the government's melting those coins down also, the

Professor's gold and silver coins would now be of really unbelievable value!

The elusive professor's use of a thin lead liner in his pouches has probably contributed to them not being found in modern times with all the electronic gadgets around except if the pouches have gotten torn in some way over the years by soil action and ground movements, new landscaping projects, or excavations.

Centennial Hall
University of Arizona

Figure 2: Centennial Hall

Centennial Hall is home to two ghosts; one is a young Spanish man from the Colonial Period of Tucson's history and is usually dressed entirely or mostly in black, and a female ghost from a later era that prefers the classic long, billowing dresses of the 1890's. Sounds from a piano can often be heard very late at night as well as frequent seemingly muffled conversations taking place often in many of the large buildings unused and empty rooms that have not been used since the 1920's.

"Yes, there are reports of two ghostly entities inhabiting Centennial Hall Theatre (the original structure here was called the Main Campus Auditorium) at the University of Arizona in Tucson, Arizona," said Jonathan Holden with U A Presents at the University of Arizona.

"There has been a building here where Centennial Hall is now located for over seventy years, they just built the new theatre over the school's original main auditorium, and it seems the ghost stories go back even farther than that to the time of the Spanish Colonial Period in Tucson.

It seems on the current site of the Centennial Hall Theatre two dashing headstrong young men visiting from Spain had settled a disagreement over a young girl's affections, after one challenged the other to a duel while they were in Tucson.

As was the custom then, the other was allowed to choose the weapons, and much to surprise of the other he chose lances on horseback much like a medieval joust except that no one but themselves knew that this challenge was clearly meant to be to the death.

Sadly, the very young and emotional girl ran out to stop them as they were in full stride on their horses and was trampled to death under the hooves of the young men's horses. Some of the townspeople's dogs began barking at the sounds of her screams causing one of the young duelers to get thrown from his horse slamming right onto the desert floor.

Tragically, he landed on the ground right on the side of his head and it snapped his neck killing him right there almost instantly. The citizens of the Presidio San Augustine del Tucson were so upset at the turn of events that they all then completely ignored the surviving young man. He soon left Tucson in complete dishonor and was not long after tortured then killed by a band of Apache Indians on his journey back south through Sonora eventually to board a Spanish Galleon sailing ship back to Spain at the busy Port of Veracruz. "

One of the ghostly entities reported at Centennial Hall on various occasions is a woman completely dressed in her 1890's Victorian era dark floor length clothing who pushes theatre customers on stairways and in open areas as if trying to quickly pass them. She is always seen wearing a late 1800's blouse with a very high collar that was the style of the era; a Cameo Pendant that was the style of that time; along with her hair pinned up as was the fashion for women during most of the 1800's.

It's often reported that she is always seen exclusively at classical performances at the theatre. Holden said actors have also often reported hearing noises directly above them while they were on the stage.

"A Spanish male spirit entity dressed entirely in dark or black clothing of another era, in his 20's has often been reported lurking and moving around backstage and he has frequently been seen up above walking along in the catwalks overhead.

He has been heard to be making horse like whining noises."

Holden added, "There is a very old adage that says in every good theatre that has live performances it almost always sightings and experiences with ghosts."

That just seems to be true when a few months ago at the theatre, an employee at the university had the most recent of the many various reported ghostly encounters there in the building both during the daytime as well as at night time. Herb Stratford, a student employee of the theater related that the employee, who was a movie projectionist, had noticed some balled up pieces of used masking tape that suddenly started to move on top of one of the work counters right near him.

"All of a sudden it started to crinkle, with the eerie sound like somebody was grabbing it. He (the employee) said out loud, 'If you're going to play with it, then play with it.' The employee then saw [the ball of tape] roll across the table and back," said Stratford.

That's not all; something was manipulating equipment in the seventy-seven-year old theatre.

Stratford said, "We'd come in the next day and the lens would be all the way screwed out; something that requires a tool to do it, there is just no other possible way it could come out. Yet there were no marks on the lens whatsoever" he said.

University of Arizona investigators also examined the lens but were unable to find any marks on it anywhere, nor could there even be found a single fingerprint or even a partial fingerprint on it. After being unofficially but thoroughly examined in the crime lab in Phoenix by a technician, the lens mysteriously did not reveal any shred of human DNA either.

Sounds from a piano can be heard late at night as well as muffled conversations taking place in empty rooms. The spirit of a woman in a long, white dress is said to haunt the now sealed off balcony area and the green room. An angry woman, she has been known to push employees. Reputed to be haunted by both a male and female ghost.

The female gets the blame for all the nasty bits of ghosting (of course) while the male ghost is seen as a more benign presence. Supposedly the female ghost is prone to pushing people down the stairs. Also, a man who some think was a patron who died of a heart attack wanders the hall, as well. The man seems to be the counter balance and helps anyone who has been injured by the woman. There is a ghost of a young man dressed in black in the balcony area. This apparition has been seen ducking through the stage entrance.

Maricopa Resident Hall
University of Arizona

There are many tales of ghosts and

Figure 3: Maricopa Resident Hall, University of Arizona

unexplainable phenomena circulating the University of Arizona[1]. With a campus that's cluttered with old, brick buildings and plumbed with state-of-the-ancient toilets

---

[1] From Myth or Reality? Ghosts at the UA by Nathan Tafoya, Arizona Daily Wildcat, Friday, October 31, 2003.

and faucets, that might not be surprising. Within the UA community, encounters with the supernatural have become as unpredictable as running into a creepy pervert.

One the University 0of Arizona's most infamous stories is about the ghost of Maricopa Residence Hall. Urban legend has it that a resident killed herself there. The circumstances surrounding her death, however, change depending on the person talking about it.

Susan Metzger, an art history senior and former Maricopa resident, said the story she heard was based on the premise of the hall being the UA president's mansion.

"The version I heard was that his daughter was engaged to be married and she found her fiancé with another woman, and so she hung herself," Metzger said. "I've heard it was on the third floor and I've heard it was on the second floor and I've heard it was in the basement. So it's random."

The hall was first proposed by UA President Arthur Herbert Wilde in 1914 and constructed between 1918 and 1921; however, it was never the president's mansion.

"I've never seen the ghost when I lived here," Metzger said. "My friend Danielle said she saw her, but I think she was drunk."

Maricopa's basement is no tipsy joke though. "The basement here is really, really scary," Metzger said. "It has a bunch of locked doors. Nothing leads to anything, just storage stuff."

Associate Director of Residence Life Patrick Call has occupied the hall in past summers and said there are people who swear they have seen the ghost. "I never saw her," he said. "I would have liked to, but I never did."

OLD MAIN
UNIVERSITY OF ARIZONA

Figure 4: Old Main

Every old building has a good ghost story to go with it, and the University of Arizona's historic Old Main is no exception.

The UA's first building, Old Main has since 1891 served as the "front porch" of the UA, and it holds special significance for generations of Wildcat alumni and campus community members. But as the iconic Old

Main underwent the most comprehensive renovation in its history, some construction crew members are reporting ghostly goings-on.

"I can't say I've seen anything, but I've heard some weird stuff as far as creaking and cracking," said Fred Briscoe, senior project manager with Sundt Construction. "We joke quite a bit that we're making Carlos mad."

The Carlos he's referring to is Carlos Maldenado, who is said to have been murdered while supervising the construction of Old Main in the 1800s.

The legend of Carlos is detailed online at www.uofamystery.org, a website not affiliated with the University.

The story goes that Carlos often spent the night at Old Main while it was being built, chatting with members of local Indian tribes who stopped by to check out the project and keeping watch over the building, which some locals were not happy to see being constructed.

One morning, Carlos's construction crew members arrived to find their beloved boss sitting in a wooden chair with a large knife stuck in his throat. His murder was never solved, and it's said that his spirit still haunts the building, where a number of students, staff and faculty have reported seeing him over the years.

Word of Carlos traveled fast among workers who are currently renovating Old Main, a project scheduled for completion in the summer of 2014.

Sundt Construction foreman Tomás Avilez certainly believes the legend. In fact, he enthusiastically claims to have seen Carlos twice, in the form of a shadowy figure in the attic of Old Main.

"He doesn't stand still long enough to take a picture," Avilez said. "He kind of hides."

"I'm not afraid of him, because I'm not afraid of stuff like that, but if you sit in the attic long enough, he might appear," he said.

Carpenter Frank Contreras also has been spooked by the ghost story.

After hearing Avilez and other colleagues talking about Carlos, he went online to do some investigating of his own and found the tale.

Not long after, he arrived at Old Main early one morning, the first one on the site. When he entered an upstairs hallway, several faucets suddenly turned on at once, sending him in the opposite direction.

Contreras's strategy, should he ever come face to face with Carlos: "Start running!"

Senior project superintendent Dennis Manley has had some frayed nerves courtesy of Carlos, too.

"I was here a lot by myself the first couple of weeks, and I'm a scaredy cat. When I came into work in the morning it was dark and I got goose bumps," he said.

But Manley is no longer worried. "Now that he sees this place is getting a facelift, I think he's gone." Old Main's custodian, Andy Martinez, has heard more than just rumors during his late night shifts cleaning the UA's oldest building. Martinez said he has seen clocks fall off of the wall and heard water fountains recharge when he was the only person in the creaky building. But one thing in particular has given him the chills every night for the past month and a half.

Martinez said around 10 p.m. one night, he was standing next to a wall on the second floor, when he heard a knock. Martinez said he stood still for a moment and looked at the glass door leading outside, knowing all the doors behind him were locked. He did not see anyone. Then he heard a second knock.

"I knew nobody was at the door and I knew nobody was here," he said. "And of course there's nobody back there. I mean, it's just storage." Martinez pointed behind the wall located in the heart of the building. Martinez said he stood still in the hallway again, looking at the wall until he heard a third knock.

"And I was like, "Wait a minute, I know I'm not hearing things,'" he said. Martinez then yelled at the unknown knocker to come in, and the knocking stopped. Since that night, Martinez said he gets freaked out when he passes by the area.

MARRONEY THEATER UNIVERSITY OF ARIZONA

Figure 5:Marroney Theater

Some ghosts give a more theatrical performance when they decide to spook members of the UA community. Some of these performances are given at the Marroney Theater. The Marroney Theatre was built in 1956. It is a 332-seat proscenium auditorium that was refurbished in 1993 with new seats, carpeting, stage drapes, lighting system and sound system.

"There are reportedly ghosts throughout the Marroney Theatre that I've had a few encounters with and that students have had encounters with as well," said theatre arts associate professor Jeff Warburton.

Warburton said a number of students have seen "Gene the Ghost" during theatrical performances.

Gene Lafferty was Warburton's predecessor, whom Warburton replaced as technical director. Warburton said he has heard steps in the theatre when he was there by himself and has experienced cold gusts of air brush over him.

One time, he lost his keys and was alone in the auditorium when he heard his keys fall from an audience seat. From jinxed productions like "The Crucible," to bad omens and phrases like "break a leg," the stage has always been a little superstitious.

"I think artists are more sensitive than people," Warburton said, explaining why this might be. But he does not believe ghosts hurt anyone. "They're not harmful at all," he said. "You usually hurt yourself running like hell."

Other scary campus stories have a lighter tone to them. Some students in the stadium residence halls have designated room 480 to "Harry the Ghost."

According to Michelle Ruppelt, a nutritional sciences junior, room 480 is an unfinished facility not large enough to be a dorm room and too small to be anything else.

"It was kind of a joke," Ruppelt said. "There's supposedly an unidentified ghost running around."

Ruppelt said the stadium residence halls have empty elevator shafts and unexplainable drafts and noises, which add to an overall feeling of eeriness. She said has not seen anything supernatural though.

English Building
University of Arizona

In many cases hauntings are caused not by something that happened in the current location, but by something that happened years ago before the current building that occupies that space was even though about. This is the case with the haunting of

Figure 6: English Building, University of Arizona

the English Building at the University of Arizona.

Where the English Building stands now used to be a running track years ago. The body of a woman that had been raped and murdered was found dumped into in a well that was at the edge of the track.

Now night custodians have seen the apparition of a woman. This figure is often seen through the windows of the locked building late at night, running, with a panicked look on her face, perhaps still trying to escape her attacker.

University of Arizona: Modern Language Building

The skeleton and ghost of an early 1900's era beautiful young woman with her very long dark hair that is sometimes pinned up and at other times can be seen flowing all the way down her back still haunts the University of Arizona's Modern Language Building that was built over the top of the site of the original Woman's Athletic Field at the University of Arizona according to persistent and continuing reported sightings over many years.

A ghost, known as the "Woman in White" haunts the Modern Language building. It's speculated that this apparition is the ghost of a young woman who was murdered on this site. She appears as a dark-haired young woman who wears a 1920s-era shawl and a long skirt. She has been seen peeking through the small window in the Romance Languages lab. When the Modern Language Building was built in 1965 workers were said to have discovered human remains. The construction workers did not report the human remains for fear that investigation would delay the project.

According to the numerous reports over the decades, the mysterious female spirit taking her ghostly form is often still seen wearing a long flowing shawl of the type not seen since the early 1910's along with a dark colored floor length with a high collar dress that was commonly worn by women between the time of 1899 and 1904. The ghost of the young lady is still reported being seen peering through and out the windows of the Romance Languages Lab and in the Modern Languages Building itself late during the night. The students who have noticed her, and then have tried to speak to her, have all said that anytime when she is addressed, she turns suddenly, then very quickly runs away every time... only to seemingly vanish into the darkness of the night right while she is still running. Interviews with those who have seen the apparition all report it is as if she was just swallowed up by the darkness of night itself!

According to various newspaper reports of the early 1900's, one night the mysterious woman was assaulted, murdered, thrown down into one of the University's deep hand dug open water wells left over from the area's use by the Spanish in the 1700's. Her body then was found floating in the water well located on the University's original athletic field early one morning by Hiram Winstead the head groundskeeper for the college. The many reports that have surfaced over the years seem to unquestionably confirm the mysterious ghost of the lady returned to the campus to search for and collect her now scattered bones in hope of giving her spirit some final peace after the unspeakable and horrendous crimes against her on that ill-fated night in the darkness.

The current Modern Language Building's location was constructed right directly over the top of the site in the year 1965. Construction workers there on the worksite were said to have found a full set of human bones there as they excavated and prepared the foundation footings but didn't report finding the skeleton/bones to anyone out of fear that the resulting investigation would delay or ultimately stop the project completely, and put them all out of work.

The ghostly apparition continues to attempt the recovery of her bones so she can move on to the next dimension that she so desperately seeks ever since but so far that goal has been elusive. It is said that if any living person(s) can ever help the ghost find her well-deserved peace she will reveal the location of something very valuable that is buried somewhere within the 1910 boundaries of what was then the University in the final moments as she transitions beyond the current netherworld she has been trapped in.

According to available records and statements made later, it is somewhat murky exactly what the workers actually did with the human bones, but it is sure that some of them did split the bones up between themselves as souvenirs, took them home and hid them, and kept them as souvenirs of the project. Of the workers on the project twenty-four of them over time died very mysterious deaths, and not one of them lived past the age of 50 years old.

There is a persistent and substantiated rumor that a fraternity house member at the University of Arizona during the mid-1960's had stolen and thus gained possession of at least some of the bones and they were buried secretly at the stroke of midnight in 1967 on the fraternity's grounds after a series of many persistent and very mysterious happenings continuing over and over at the fraternity. Subsequently, by 1974 the fraternity had its charter revoked losing it's building in the process. The fraternity's original building was itself leveled for a commercial structure and asphalt parking lot which is now located directly over the top of where the fraternity house had originally stood.

Further information over the years has confirmed that a small group of University of Arizona Alumnus from the mid 1960's to early 1970's still meet precisely at midnight once each year over the spot where some of the murdered girls bones now are buried. In a still well guarded secret ceremony using a well a memorized chant form the former college students continue asking for forgiveness of the actions of the fraternity brother who originally stole the skeleton's bones which seemingly brought the bad fortune to them all perpetually, and as some say put a curse (see video) (see video) on all of the fraternity's members, their offspring, and all others who were either involved or did nothing to make things right on those fateful moments of time in the 1960's.

There have been numerous complaints from both past and the current property owner where the fraternity house once stood concerning attempts by a person or persons unknown to try to dig through always the same certain areas of cement, asphalt, and landscaping on the property.

The various owners and their managers have also noted a very high unexplained employee turnover, and amount of 'unusual' employee injuries at the many businesses that have occupied the property since the demolition of the fraternity structure over the ensuing years.

Surprisingly, many of the employee's injuries are exactly the same or very eerily similar to the ones experienced and reported by the members of the fraternity that was once located on the property including fractured or broken bones, sudden disorientation and falls to the ground causing injuries (see video), nightmares of drowning in water then waking up completely drenched in sweat, and the loss of fingers and toes including the bones.

Of the fraternity's members between 1965 and 1967, many have died under unusual circumstances according to the records. Beginning in the spring of 1966 two members died in vehicle related accidents after being hit by automobiles, another fraternity member was murdered then cut up into pieces with some put down the garbage disposal and the rest almost completely eaten by his insanely jealous and apparently well over the edge insane wife in New York City before she was finally arrested when neighbors reported seeing large blood stains on her clothes. Her death however very suddenly of supposedly natural causes while in jail before her trial could be scheduled was yet another continuing odd and bizarre twist in an already horrific event that seemingly consumed the woman also.

Another fraternity member died horrifically when he was working as the foreman of the electric company back in his home town he somehow got his coat's left sleeve caught in one of the fast moving conveyor belts that are automated to continually load coal up into the power company's furnaces that provided electricity to the community.

Unable to turn the automated equipment off without the foreman's key, the other employees watched in sheer horror as he was quickly carried screaming and pleading for someone to do something to help him as he was carried for just over 200 feet along on the conveyor that rose up and operated almost 45 foot off the ground.

Still alive, he was then flung like a beat up rag doll at almost 50 miles an hour into the blast furnaces that ran the generators producing the electricity that powered his entire hometown. By the nature of the occurrence not a single piece or part of any of his remains could never be recovered from the 2000+ degree hot bowels of the blast furnace.

In time five other fraternity members each met what could only be termed as untimely deaths by officials during the course of various types of what seemingly appeared to be robberies or muggings they had encountered in their lives. However, some maintained that it was the direct result of the lady's ghost who had been searching their pockets for her bones since on three of the bodies there appeared what seemed to be long deep scratches deep into their skin. Nine others died of what were termed natural causes according to autopsy records before they had even reached the age of thirty-five.

BEAR DOWN GYM

Figure 7:Bear Down Gym

The University of Arizona Wildcat's battle cry of Bear Down and fight song (hear it here) comes from the Thursday October 18, 1926 final dying words of a 22-year old wildly popular charismatic student leader, and multi-talented athlete who often trained in what was then the newly built Men's Gymnasium as the Bear Down Gym was originally named.

In 1925 John 'Button' Byrd Salmon was the President of the Student Body, the varsity football teams starting quarterback and team captain, and a three-year star catcher for the baseball team with obvious major league potential. Nicknamed 'Button' by his family for his small frame (5'8", 145 pounds) and unbelievably impish good looks, he was extremely popular with his teammates, coach, fellow students, the people of Tucson, all the schools girls, and many of the young girls around town.

In 1925, the year just before his untimely death, John 'Button' Byrd Salmon completely amazed a stadium crowd of over 30,000 University of Southern California (USC) Trojan fans as well as his University of Arizona supporters up in the stands at the game against USC in 1925 Los Angeles with his almost superhuman powerful punts, literally flying over the top of opponents, and totally fearless defensive plays. This was one very talented athlete without fear who was a 'hard as a rock kid' with his wild curly reddish hair and freckles who inspired his teammates to bestow the nickname on him of 'The Leaping Tuna.'

John 'Button' Salmon was also an exceptionally talented baseball catcher with clearly major league talents. In the spring of 1925 his clutch two base hit drove in the winning run against USC in a very heated baseball game. When John 'Button' Byrd Salmon was elected the Student Body President just four days later he referred to that 'hit' as 'my 200 vote double.'

John's father, Frank Salmon was born in 1875 and raised in Texas. Frank, was an educated smart tough no nonsense but always very supportive family man who worked hard in management for the Phelps Dodge Copper Corporation in Bisbee during the Deportation of 1917, his mother Kathryn E. (Simpson) Salmon was a gentle yet tough fine lady and very loving mother born in New Orleans, Louisiana in 1878. Eventually, both parents were buried in Tucson near the son they loved so much.

Their son, John 'Button' Byrd Salmon was born in Christoval, Texas on October 22, 1903 and grew up with his parents in the tough early 1900's copper mining town of Bisbee, Arizona. 'Button's' older brother Riney B. Salmon was also very athletic, and mentored-supported his young brother John 'Button' Byrd Salmon in both baseball and football at Bisbee's Warren Ballpark where the Young 'Button' Salmon regularly played baseball with the likes of numerous members of the Chicago White Socks, and many other pro ball players of the time who spent time there in the off season. 'Button's" brother Riney B. Salmon later became the President of the Arizona-Texas Baseball League from 1948 to 1950.

The very day after the 1926 season's big opening football game, John 'Button' Byrd Salmon was driving at a very high rate of speed coming back from Phoenix in his Ford Model T with a football-fraternity buddy and a young girl when he missed a treacherous curve and hit the dirt berm along the side of the road near Picacho Peak, Arizona. His car overturned numerous times, and crashed down into a deep ravine pinning him underneath the wreckage for hours until any help arrived. The other two passengers were both ejected from the car miraculously sustaining only a few deep lacerations, cuts and bruises, but they were not seriously injured.

However, young John 'Button' Byrd Salmon was not so lucky and suffered a severed spinal cord injury leaving him paralyzed from the neck down. Dr. Victor Melsor, a well-respected and extremely talented Tucson surgeon, performed the 8-hour surgery on 'Button' at the Southern Methodist Hospital in Tucson, but the spinal injury was just too severe. John 'Button' Byrd Salmon died 14 days later on October 18, 1926, at Southern Methodist Hospital in Tucson.

On the day of October 18, 1926 'Button' gave a final message to his coach and ultimately to his football and baseball teammates. John 'Button' Salmon's coach 'Pop' Mc Kale, who had been visiting 'Button' Salmon every single day for 13 days at the hospital, was talking to 'Button' when the injured young man whispered 'Pop' come closer..."Tell them...Tell The Team To Bear Down. The Nurse in attendance then noted that John '

Button' Salmon breathed in one last breath and died peacefully at 10:32 am.

On the day of his funeral all classes at the University of Arizona and all over Tucson were cancelled for the day. Employers and employees city wide left their jobs to attend John 'Button' Byrd Salmon's funeral service which was held on the University of Arizona's campus at the auditorium. Afterwards, the well over three-mile long line of Ford Model T's, Model A's, citizens on horseback and driving horse drawn wagons, every taxi in town that was running, and various other cars of the era slowly made their way from the University of Arizona through downtown Tucson and up to the Evergreen Cemetery north out of town to the cemetery off Oracle Rd.

Late the night of October 18, 1926 after 'Pop' had returned from the hospital he was working at his office desk in Bear Down Gym around 10pm that night. It was revealed only later that the ghost of John 'Button' Byrd Salmon wearing his football jersey appeared to him at the doorway to the office and began walking toward the exhausted coach.

The apparition uttered only two words, "Bear Down." Other employees, janitor's, and students in the gym both during the day and especially late at night have reported over the years since 1926 their encountering the apparition of a short young man in a well-used 1920's era football jersey moving throughout various areas of the gym.

Constructed in 1926 to replace Herring Hall, and named after Colonel Herring, which was the university's original gymnasium, Bear Down Gym is a two story brick structure noted for its curved roof, large semicircular terra cotta entrance and deeply recessed entry with copper-clad window frames. The building is topped with a slightly projecting cornice that includes terra cotta detailing. The exposed bow-truss roofing system is a notable interior feature.

Originally, the main level provided basketball courts and room for gymnastics, while the lower level contained locker rooms, offices, and space for the Department of Military Science and Tactics. The building at one time seated about 6,000 spectators and was used for sports, school dances, and the annual student registration activities.

Quickly after December 7, 1941 with the outbreak of World War II, Bear Down Gym (and many other facilities at the U of A) were taken over by the U.S. War Department as a barracks for 500 young students at a time as they went through their "Expedited" Naval Indoctrination School, just prior to being shipped off to war. Many of the 'green' sailors and officers who lived and trained there together 24/7 gave their lives in the war effort and never returned. It's said that their ghosts still frequent Bear Down Gym looking to start where they left off back when they were young

ARIZONA STATE MUSEUM SOUTH

Figure 8: Arizona State Museum South

All of the museums at the University of Arizona are built on top of the ancient sites of the now lost (or almost) American Indian Tribes of the Hohokam, and many others in more recent times including the Apaches, Pascua Yaqui (Toltec's from ancient Mexico), Yaqui, Papago, Sand Papago, and Tohono O'Odham-"People of the Desert"- (Hohokam descendants).

At what is now the Arizona State Museum South (an archeological museum) at 1010 E. University Boulevard (the s/w side of campus) closest to the rock wall that is on Park Ave, was in 1885 at just the very extreme desert edges of the Territorial University of Arizona's property. It was the mid -1930's and the United States was deep into a world-wide economic depression that had millions of North Americans destitute, homeless, jobless, and looking for their next meals.

Tucson fared even worse than most other cities its size, and jobs were almost non-existent. As part of the U.S. Governments WPA (Works Projects Administration) Projects, some funds were allocated in 1935 to build sidewalks around Tucson and some projects at the University Of Arizona for what is known now as the Arizona State Museum South.

The economic failure of the country was so serious that in many of Tucson's families, boys between the ages of 13 to 17 were taken out of school or the home and went to work just so that the family could buy food and be able to pay the rent or mortgage before facing eviction. These boys were expected to do the same jobs of any adult working man no matter their age.

Work began in 1936 for the large scale job of digging and laying the foundation for the Arizona State Museum building most of the work was done by hand using picks and shovels. One of the crews consisted of six young men between the ages of 13 and 16. They had a hard job ahead of them digging by hand with shovels down to the foundation level, but all of them put in an outstanding effort.

Their reward was that on the West Side of the foundation their crew was chosen to put in the first section of rock and concrete foundation wall. Things that early morning started out in fine spirits as the young boys built their foundation section up to a height of about 8 feet. Then, suddenly the unthinkable happened. As the 13 to 16-year old boys were down in the trench the foundation wall section fell over on top of them crushing and killing all six of the young boys instantly.

The news spread around town quickly, and calls were heard questioning why such young boys had been down working in the deep trench at all. A few days later when work resumed, odd unexplained things began to happen to the work crews. The dead boys voices could be heard at times, tools soon seemingly disappeared into thin air, pallets of bricks fell over onto a supervisors car, cement poured one day might be found full of large cracks along its entire length the next day.

Currently the Museum located there on the campus of the University of Arizona contains and displays many exhibits featuring thousands of artifacts from Tucson's ancient residents. The first floor is open to the public with collections and exhibits. But, up on the 2nd floor both the public and employees have never been allowed any access since the opening of the massive brick and stone building as a museum.

Behind the many 2nd floor hall doors there are virtually unknown and unmarked rooms containing the largest collections of specimens in the world from all the ancient peoples of what is now called Arizona.

Student docents, regular University employees, and others have all reported for many years the many strange happenings and noises they have regularly experienced somewhat difficult to explain occurrences and sensations during their time within the old musty walls, halls, and basement of the old and apparently haunted, museum[2].

---

[2] UOFAMYSTERY.ORG

Colossal Cave

Figure 9:Colossal Cave

Colossal Cave is located at 16711 Colossal Cave Road. Artifacts confirm that Colossal Cave was used as shelter by the ancient Hohokam Indians from about 900 through 1450 AD. The peaceful Indians farmed the valley below the cave, which about a thousand years later became known as La Posta Quemada Ranch. Today the cave and ranch are united as Colossal Cave Mountain Park, a historical destination and educational outreach for school children[3].

Colossal Cave has never been fully explored. Although there are an estimated 39 miles of cave tunnels, it took over two years to map just two miles of passageway where tours penetrate six stories deep into the cave. Visitors can choose from ongoing daily "generic tours" or can arrange more adventurous tours through darkened more narrow passages requiring hardhats and good physical fitness. There are even "candlelight tours" where each visitor is given a lighted candle to experience the cave as the Hohokam did over a thousand years ago without electric-powered lights.

While the sights that can be seen inside the cave can awe the senses, there are also stories about ghosts inside Colossal Cave. One female ghost was considered a regular visitor but she must have found another place to call her own, as she hasn't been seen in a number of years. However, the next time you take a tour of the cave, keep an eye on the members of your group. Don't be surprised if an old gentleman vanishes before your eyes. He's been

---

[3] http://www.arizona-leisure.com/colossal-cave-arizona.html

seen both by employees and visitors and must be pretty content with his living quarters.

There was once a "lady in white" who haunted the cave and its entrance. This lady has not been seen in quite a while. Then here is the ghost of an Indian Maiden who, it is said, while running from a bear, entered the cave to escape only to be killed by the 12 foot drop at that original entrance. Her sobs and cries have been heard inside the cave. The ghost of Frank Schmidt, one of the developers of Colossal Cave, is said to haunt the cave. The ghost reportedly has been seen checking up on activities around the cave.

Apache Junction Sewers

There has long been a story that the Apache Junction Sewers are haunted. It is said that the ghost is that of a worker that fell down a sewer hole and drowned. He is normally seen in a work suit carrying his hat in his hand. It would be true to say that paranormal activity at the Apache Junction began as early as during the Spaniard and Indian quarrels over the mountains.

The disappearance of the Spanish miners who were later found decapitated was blamed on the Apache Indians. However, the Apaches swore that they had nothing to do with those killings and that it was the Thunder God punishing the Spaniards.

Since Waltz supposedly revealed the location of the mine, the 10,000 people who ventured out to find it have either died or vanished. There are almost 100 bodies that have been found and were either shot or their heads cut off their bodies.

Bonilla's Elementary School

Bonilla's Elementary School is located at 4757 E. Winsett. According to local legend, the first grade girls' restrooms at Bonilla's Elementary School are haunted. It is reported that inside the restroom there is a door that is always locked. Students have seen a young blonde girl in an old fashioned dress with a matching bow walk through that door even though it was locked at the time. The identity of this ghost is not known.

Catalina High School

3645 E. Pima St.
Tucson, AZ 87516

Figure 10: Catalina High School

Catalina High School is located at 3645 E. Pima Street. There have been stories about Catalina High School being haunted for a number of years. Some say at around 7:30 at night you can hear footsteps going down to the cellar and some say that you can hear light tapings on the lockers and sometimes in the locker rooms. If mad, he'll bang the lockers very viciously. Others have reported that there are spirits that haunt the bleachers on the football field. Several people have reported seeing what look like shadow people sitting on the bleachers as if watching a game. Students have reported that during school events that all bathroom stalls were locked, and many times bathrooms were closed off because of unexplainable floods.

The ghost of a school custodian, Martin Valencia is said to haunt the school. While working at the school in the 1970s, Valencia suffered a heart attack and died on the job. The ghost of Valencia was reportedly seen cleaning the restrooms in June 1980 before the graduation ceremonies. Trash containers and cleaning supplies disappear and turn up other places and doors slam shut and lights turn off.

Kino Community Hospital

The University Medical Center (formerly

Figure 11: Kino Community Hospital

Kino Community Hospital) is located at 2800 E Ajo Way. A spirit called "George" is said to haunt the hospital. George gets blamed for pulling out chairs;

he has been seen in the hospital basement right before disappearing into the solid wall.

There are also a number of stories about the Kino Community Hospital being haunted by a former patient. One pharmacy tech had the scare of his life one evening. At that time, the pharmacy was located in the basement. The pharmacy is always locked for security reasons and only pharmacy staff can get inside. The building itself was only a few years old at the time.

On this particular occasion, it was a busy Saturday night, about 8 pm. The pharmacist was in the IV room making a TPN. The tech was filling medicine orders. Suddenly, feeling watched, the tech turned around and saw a patient watching him about 30 feet away. What was so strange was that the unknown individual was actually inside the locked pharmacy.

He then walked to the tech's right and disappeared behind the shelving. The tech ran over to the shelves, but the patient was gone. There was no place for him to hide and nowhere else he could have gone. The tech summoned the pharmacist and asked her if she saw him. She hadn't but told the tech that it was probably George, a resident ghost who frequently shows up around the hospital and has been known to pull chairs out as well. Or perhaps that is a second ghost. Apparently all the hospital staff knows about George."

LI'L ABNER STEAKHOUSE

Figure 12: Li'l Abner's Steak House

Li'l Abner Steakhouse is located at 8500 N. Silverbell Road. Lil Abner's Steakhouse in Tucson is a great old place to eat, great food, great atmosphere and a ghost that leaves the customers alone. The area is an old one, originally it was the Butterfield Express Stage Stop in the early 1800s. Lil Abner's opened up as a restaurant and bar in 1947.

There are a number of stories that there are various ghosts that haunt this building. Muffled conversations and knocking on the doors are heard. One ghost dates from when this building was an eyeglass factory. The ghost is an ex-factory worker who is looking for his lost eyeglasses.

The ghost is not from the long past of the restaurant, but is from the 90's and once worked there at the restaurant. The Ghost is named George and used to be a maintenance man at the restaurant. George, perhaps maintaining his work etiquette does not bother the customers, and is considerably shy. The employees at Lil Abner's have seen George and have even heard him as well. Apparently he would drive every so often to Mexico, but before he would go he would always have a large Coke at the bar. Some have seen him, dressed in all white, standing at the bar and drinking a large coke, disappearing moments later. Some hear things falling behind the bar and their names being called out only to find themselves all alone.

George apparently also loved to eat Cap'n Crunch Cereal. People have heard a crunching sound coming from his old room, almost like he is still enjoying some of his favorite old cereal. All in all, however, George is a harmless ghost, a friendly one and will not interfere with customers enjoying the good food they find at Lil Abner's.

Other employees though feel that there are others haunting the area and have heard whispered voices and loud knocking on doors that have nobody behind them. Whatever the case that doesn't stop the restaurant from firing up the mesquite grill and cooking up some great steaks. Stop in for a spell, and order a large coke.

Luz Academy Of Tucson

The Luz Academy of Tucson which is located at 2797 N. Introspect Dr. Tucson, AZ, 85745 occupies the building that use to house the Desert Hills Behavioral Treatment Center.

There are numerous rumors about deaths on the grounds of the school, at least one of which has been confirmed. Some report seeing a middle aged woman with long curly black hair wandering the hallways. There are also reports that there is the spirit of a young boy that appears trapped in the building and is unable to get out. Lights switching on and off, voices and other noises can be heard in many areas of the school.

Tucson Medical Center Education Building

There are stories that maintain that the Education Building at TMC (Tucson Medical Center) is one of the most haunted buildings in Tucson. Its history dates back to 1930's. The building is two stories, though originally, the first floor was used as a stable for horses. The second story had rooms to live in for student nurses and the people who took care of the horses.

One woman, who was a well-respected nurse, died of an un-known disease. Now her ghost haunts the hallways on the second floor of what is now known as the education building. Another ghost that haunts the education building was a older man who took care of the horses. One night he stayed in the stables late to clean them and was stabbed with a pitchfork. No one knew who murdered the guy.

People have reported seeing figures of both the nurse and the older man. The nurse, who is also known as "The Lady in White" likes to greet people by talking to them and by helping them open doors.

The man, also known as "The Cold Spirit," likes to make people feel as uncomfortable as possible. When it is cold outside, he likes to turn the heater off after someone has just turned it on. When it is hot out, he likes to turn off the air conditioning after someone has just put it on. He also likes to slam doors and throw objects across the room. This ghost haunts the 1st floor where the stables were.

This is an interesting building because when you walk in you can feel the energy all around you. It is scary and a creepy place."

Bloom Elementary

Figure 13: Bloom Elementary School

Bloom Elementary School is located as 8310 E. Pima Street. According to witnesses there are several spirits who are said to haunt this location. The principle of Bloom Elementary passed away inside the school and ever since then there have been reports of many weird experiences, like a brick falling out of a wall in the bathroom, door unlocking them self's, and some people have even seen the deceased principal walking about the halls. Doors lock and unlock and there are various other apparitions that have been reported.

Collier Elementary School

There have been witnesses at Collier Elementary School that have reported seeing the bodies of children hanging in the middle of the halls by ropes. There have also been mysterious things happen like doors closing immediately when it is not windy at all and the sound of footsteps being heard in empty rooms. Some witnesses have even seen Mrs. Collier, after whom the school is named walking around the building.

Davis Bilingual School

Figure 14: Davis Bilingual School

William C Davis was a Tucson pioneer, coming to Tucson in 1869 and opening a very successful hardware store. He was also fundamental in the founding of the First National Bank of Tucson. He, like many others in the territory, was also interested in the mining business and the boom towns, he invested heavily in several mining situations. Davis went on to serve as a Pima County Supervisor and in the Territorial Legislature. He became interested in the public school system and at intervals from 1872 until 1902 he served on the School Board of Tucson District 1.

The Davis Bilingual School, built in 1901 was originally constructed with only five rooms.

Though renovated and expanded many times, the age of the building seems to be a factor in the many paranormal events and sightings that have taken place inside its walls. At dawn the figure of a woman appears in the classrooms, but only at dawn. Parents have felt someone touching them on the shoulder.

Students have heard eerie music in the halls, and doors that are locked have become unlocked and open on their own. Students have seen water faucets, even non-sensored faucets, turn on slowly until they reach full blast, and then turn off by themselves. During the most recent reported event, students saw a water faucet turn on slowly then full blast. Next they saw the actual water faucet handle turn itself off.

Desert View High School

There has long been a story about a young boy was killed at Desert View High School by a person or persons unknown (some have whispered about an unknown creature being the culprit). The spirit of the child is now said to be haunting the school.

Desert View Ranch

There is a young girl dressed in prairie clothes wearing a white apron that wanders in the area where the old chicken coop and horse corral were located at Desert View Ranch. She is said to have died from a fever. She will sometimes laugh and be seen standing by an old tree. Younger children will talk of her and have said her name is Lillian.

Evergreen Cemetery

Figure 15: A private crypt at Evergreen Cemetery

Evergreen Cemetery is located at 3015 North Oracle Road in Tucson. Evergreen Cemetery lies at the foot of Mount Rubidoux in Riverside, California. This historic cemetery was founded in 1872 and has not only historic grave sites but many from the various wars in which this country has fought.

There are more than 27,000 beings interred on this site, many of regional and national significance. More than 1,500 lie in the historic portion of Evergreen. Among them are Riverside's most notable founders: However, it must be said that not every resident of this historic graveyard rests easily. Visitors to Evergreen Cemetery have reported hearing the voices of young children laughing and talking in the cemetery when no one is around. Some have reported feeling that negative presences at certain times.

Fox Theater

Figure 16:Fox Theater

The Fox Tucson Theatre opened on April 11, 1930 as a dual vaudeville/movie house. The Fox featured a stage, full fly-loft, and dressing rooms beneath the stage. The combined effects of "talkies" and the Depression limited the opportunities for live performance, and the dressing rooms were never completed.

Opening night, April 11, 1930, proved to be the biggest party the small community of Tucson had ever seen. With Congress Street closed and waxed for dancing, four live bands, a live radio broadcast and free trolley rides downtown, the party was one not to be missed. So began Fox's 40-year reign as the "crown jewel" of downtown Tucson's entertainment world. Originally, the Fox served as Tucson's Movie Palace, presenting films on the big screen in addition to community events, vaudeville performances and the Tucson Chapter of the Mickey Mouse Club.

Competition for new theaters and the decline of downtown shopping led to the Fox closing in 1974. After sitting empty for 25 years, the theater was nearly beyond restoration. Extensive water damage, vandalism, and neglect had conspired to keep the building dark. The owners, who had decided to let the building slowly decay, had little interest in selling the property to anyone. Following a two-year negotiation, the non-profit Fox Tucson Theatre Foundation was able to purchase the building in 1999 for $250,000.

Stabilization and planning for the rehabilitation/restoration began at once with a new roof being installed to stop further damage from the elements. Small restoration projects such as the repair and relighting of the original chandeliers kept the community engaged—through bi-annual open houses and special event fund-raisers.

Following a six year, $14 million rehabilitation the theatre reopened on New Year's Eve 2006 (12/3/05). The building is listed as on the National Register of Historic Places due to its unique "Southwestern Art Deco" decor as well as it world class acoustics. The impact of the reopened of the Fox Tucson Theatre on downtown, the larger community of Tucson, and on Southern Arizona as a whole, has been profound.

In 2013, the Fox hosted over 150 events and saw over 70,000 patrons through its door. The 1164 seat audience capacity is big enough to attract national and international talent, yet small enough to boast an intimate entertainment experience. Once again the Fox is a premier performance venue, a classic film buff's dream (showing classic 35mm films on the big screen "the way they were meant to be seen"), and a multi-purpose, elegant rental facility for corporate, non-profit and private events. No one knows who the ghost might be, but a strange man dressed up from the 1920's has been seen around the Fox Theater. He will ask for money to feed his family that is suffering from The Great Depression. The Fox Theatre's projection room is reportedly haunted by a past projectionist who can't let go of his job. Another spirit seen roaming the halls of the Fox is that of a man who was killed while helping build the theater. The wooden board he was working on before he passed is still just partially installed in the theater's ceiling due to no one wanting to fix it after his death.

Fred G. Acosta Job Corps Center

Figure 17" Fred G. Acosta Job Corp Center

The Fred G. Acosta Job Corp Center is located on Campbell Avenue in Tucson. It is the mission of the Fred G. Acosta Job Corps Center to create a pathway of economic success for disadvantaged youth through a career service delivery system. Many of those who train at the Center stay in the Dormitory which is home to 195 students. The lobby separating the male and female wings is spacious, attractive and offers opportunities for students to congregate in a pleasant, mutual setting for conversation, enjoying movies and meeting friends.[4]

Unfortunately, it would that some of those who call the dormitory home do not want to leave. There are reports that at around 5 am, all of the toilets in the first floor female dormitory bathroom flush by themselves.

Students have also reported seeing a girl playing with a ball in the female side second floor dormitory. It is also reported that at about midnight in the 2nd bathroom that the showers turn on and off by themselves. There have been a number of rumors that a girl who used frequent the Center slit her wrists and drowned herself in the tub in the 2nd floor bathroom. It is also reported that some of

---

[4] This information came from the Fred G. Acosta Job Corp Center website. http://fredgacosta.jobcorps.gov/html/inside/?pid=campus

those who stay at the dormitory sometimes have dreams about this particular girl. Finally, on the fifth floor, in room 509, there is a strange light that seems to suddenly appear in the room, but them fades away.

Garcia's Restaurant

Garcia's Restaurant is housed in the old El Paso Southwest Railroad Depot building. It was in this old railroad yard that Wyatt Earp is said to have murdered Frank Stillwell for what he believed was Stillwell's involvement in the ambush shooting of

Figure 18: Inside Garcia's Restaurant

Wyatt's brother Morgan Earp in Tombstone.

Housed in the old El Paso and South West railroad depot, Garcia's makes good use of a historic building that might have otherwise gone abandoned. It is also the site of several other murders throughout the years. The basement still contains remnants of the jail where prisoners were kept while awaiting transportation.

However, the shooting of Stillwell by Earp is by far the most famous incident. After the ambush of Morgan Earp, a posse had failed to find those responsible for the dastardly deed, but Wyatt Earp had his strong suspicions. He believed, and perhaps rightly so that the Earps and their friends were marked for death by the Clanton faction.

According to the later statements of Ike Clanton, Ike Clanton and Frank Stilwell were at the Tucson train station to meet a witness in a trial coming in on the same train. Sitting under the veranda of the Porter Hotel, Stillwell told Clanton that the Earps were on the train and he didn't want any trouble. According to Clanton's later testimony, they walked about a block away near a school and continued to talk.

The Earps finished dinner and walked back to the train that was to take the crippled Virgil Earp and Morgan Earp's body to California for burial.

Doc had a shorter man, probably McMasters, retrieve the shotguns and they escorted Virgil and Allie onto the train. At this point, Wyatt spotted Stillwell. In one version both Stillwell and Clanton are spotted on flat cars on a side track looking for a clear shot at the Earps. Wyatt claimed he saw the glint of a rifle barrel.

Wyatt and his friends then got off the train and walked back toward the Porter Hotel down the left side of the train. Frank Stillwell came back from the school and came around the northwest corner of the hotel to take in the scene. He may actually have intended to take a shot at the Earps.

Frank saw Wyatt and his men advancing towards him but didn't think they were going to attack him as it was no secret that Wyatt and his men were going to take an eastbound train back to Contention and Tombstone, while Virgil and his wife went on to California. So Frank could have believed Wyatt and his men were coming back to the Porter Hotel. When he finally realized he was marked for death after seeing that Wyatt had spotted him in the shadows and was now running toward him but that he was now running towards his position, Frank panicked and started running down the tracks, probably angling across them to get out in the desert.

After a hundred yards (a saloon keeper, George Hand said it was 200 yards), Wyatt caught up with Stilwell, who turned and perhaps thought he could surrender. Wyatt walked right up him, stuck the shotgun in his belly, just under the heart and pulled both triggers. According to Wyatt, Stillwell yelled, "Morg!" as he was shot, perhaps a reference to Morgan Earp who had been assassinated mere days prior to this. He always believed Stilwell was in on the shooting of Wyatt's favorite brother.

According to one version of the story after Doc Holliday and the others ran up and each took turns shooting holes in Stilwell's body. By chasing down Stilwell, they had missed the eastbound train's departure and Wyatt knew it was only a matter of time before they were found out. Clearly outside the law, and desperate to get away, they ran down the tracks, perhaps expecting a Bob Paul posse to catch up with them at any moment. They ran and walked 11 miles down the tracks towards Benson and finally, illegally flagged down an eastbound freight train at midnight. Arriving back in Tombstone a wanted man (Sheriff Bob Paul had wired Tombstone for the sheriff to arrest Wyatt) John Behan tried to arrest Wyatt but that's another confrontation.

A number of guests and staff at Garcia's have reported phenomenon that includes unusual smells, apparition like figures and unexplainable noises.

Francis Owen Holaway Elementary School

Figure 19: Francis Owen Holaway Elementary School

Francis Owen Holaway Elementary School is located on N. Cherry Avenue in Tucson. While the school building is not all that old, it was built in

1957, there have been a number of sightings of a figure believed to be that of Mr. Holaway himself who has been seen by janitors checking the classrooms at around 11 or 12 at night.

It's said that the janitor was waking the school corridor on his way to clean one of the rooms when he saw a figure of a man trying to unlock a door. Knowing that no one was supposed to be in the building but himself the janitor called out to the man, but received no answer. Concerned that here might have been a break in, the janitor attempted to confront the unknown figure, but as he reached the doorway that the unknown person was trying to open, the man simply faded away.

Hooters Restaurant, Gotham and The New West Nightclub[5]

Staff and guests that have eaten at Hooter's Restaurant, Gotham or the New West Nightclub have reported seeing strange presences and feeling unusual energies. There have been reports of cold chills and the strong presence of a spirit who would

---

[5]Gotham and the New West are both closed down now due to a gang-related shooting that led to someone's death.

follow staff as they moved throughout the back part of the club.

A former worker at the club for a long time says he was working the closing shift one evening. He and a few other employees were finishing up for the night on one particular evening. It was around three or four in the morning and he had his back facing the front door when all of a sudden he felt the sensation of a human being coming right toward him!

He turned around and immediately swung out his fist instinctively. He says that nobody was there but he had the strangest feeling that "something" went right through him.

Hotel Congress

Figure 20: Hotel Congress

The Hotel Congress was built in 1919 to serve the needs of the growing cattle industry as well as the many passengers of the Southern Pacific. The Hotel Congress of the 1920s was the perfect shelter for genteel travelers and high-rollers fresh from the east. It might have continued as just another place of lodging for road weary guests, if not for the date of January 22, 1934 has forever stamped its historical mark upon this edifice.

A fire started on the basement of the hotel and spread up the elevator shaft on the third floor.

This fire led to the capture of one the country's most notorious criminals John Dillinger. After a series of bank robberies, the Dillinger Gang had come to Tucson to lay low. The gang resided on the third floor under aliases. After the desk clerk contacted them through the switchboard[6] the gang members escaped by aerial ladders.

On the urgent request of the gang, and encouraged by a generous tip, two firemen retrieved their heavy luggage. It was later discovered that the bags contained a small arsenal of weapons as well as $23,816 in cash. Later these same two firemen recognized the gang in a true detective magazine. A stakeout ensued and the gang members were captured at a house on North Second Ave in the space of five hours, without firing a single shot. To the embarrassment of the federal authorities, the police of small town Tucson had done what the combined forces of several states and the FBI had tried so long to do. When captured, Dillinger simply muttered, "Well, I'll be damned".

However, along with being associated with the capture of John Dillinger, the Hotel Congress is

---

[6] The original switchboard is still in operation at the hotel.

also associated with several ghosts. One of the rooms in the hotel is haunted by a man who had a heart attack and died. He has been seen looking out of the window.

Room 242 is known as the Suicide Room, a name given to it a few years ago, when a troubled woman shot herself in the bathroom after a standoff with the police and a SWAT team. People staying in this room often hear strange noises that are quite creepy and they often have nightmares involving bloody suicides. The ghost of this woman has also been seen in the bathroom and in the hallway outside of her room.

The spirit of a man who passed away from a heart attack has been seen peeking from one of the windows here.

A cowboy's ghost has been seen in the basement.

A female ghost dressed in Victorian Clothing is seen on the stairwell or in the lobby. When she appears there is a distinctive scent of roses.

The ghost of a man with the initials "T.S." is often seen on the second floor. "T.S." died in a gunfight that arose from an argument over a card game in the Hotel Congress's lobby. This ghost is always dressed in an old-fashioned gray suit and frequently seen peeking out of the upper floor windows.

A permanent resident of the hotel still haunts the place. "Vince" lived in the hotel for 36 years, since his death in 2001 he haunts the place. Employees have found butter knives from the hotel's Cup Café in difference places on the second floor. Vince carried a butter knife that he would use as a screwdriver.

Hotel housekeepers who were cleaning up room 214 would have their vacuum cleaner plug pulled constantly. They learned though that if they turned on a radio that was playing music from the 1920s they would be left in peace while they were cleaning.

A cold spot and dark shadow appear in front of room 242, it is believed to be the remnants of a young lady who committed suicide on that floor. In room 240 it is said that sometimes if you look out the window you don't see modern Tucson but an old train, stagecoaches and horses. It was also reported that a bloody handprint was seen in this room.

Old Jail

People have seen ghost in old style jail uniforms at the Old Jail. According to local legend, in the 1800s a woman named Mary-Sue was arrested for a murder that she didn't commit. She was so despondent over being arrested that she hung herself by a rope inside the jail.

Later in 1830s they found out she was not the killer after a man named John was caught in the act killing another person and the finger prints match the same killing.

Old Tucson Studios

Old Tucson Studios is southern Arizona's premier outdoor entertainment venue with a full array of live shows, legendary gunfights, thrilling stunts, saloon musicals and stagecoach adventures, plus a variety of rides, food, shopping and fun for the whole family. From western movie heroes like John Wayne to current box-office stars such as Harrison Ford, many of Hollywood's legends have walked these rugged streets, the setting for hundreds of major motion pictures. Annually, this former movie studio is visited by more than 350,000 guests who visit the park each year to retrace the footsteps of their favorite stars and spend a day in the life of an 1880's western town.

Figure 21: Town Hall and gallows

"City Hall" Old Tucson Studios came to life in 1939 when Columbia Pictures chose a Pima County-owned site on which to build a replica of
The Lone Ranger and the Lost City of Gold (1957), and *Cimarron* (19591860's Tucson for the

movie Arizona. The $2.5 million film, starring William Holden and Jean Arthur, set a new standard of realism for Hollywood westerns, initiating the move away from studio backdrop movies to outdoor epics.

Local technicians and carpenters built the town from scratch, erecting more than 50 buildings in 40 days. Descendants of the Tohono O'odham, Arizona's first inhabitants formerly known as the Papago, assisted in the set production. Without the convenience of running water, they made more than 350,000 adobe bricks from the desert dirt to create authentic structures for the film. Many of those structures still stand today.

After the filming of Arizona, Old Tucson Studios lay dormant under the desert sun. The studio was revived only briefly for the films The Bells of St. Mary's (1945), starring Bing Crosby and Ingrid Bergman. Hollywood then began taking notice of Old Tucson Studios, which soon became a favorite filming location, being referred to as "Hollywood in the Desert." In 1947, Gene Autry starred in *The Last Roundup*, followed in 1950 by Jimmy Stewart in *Winchester '73*, and Ronald

Reagan in *The Last Outpost*. During the 1950's, the Western movie era was in full swing nationwide. In the fifties alone, such western classics as *Gunfight at the OK Corral* (1956) with Burt Lancaster and Kirk Douglas,) with Glenn Ford were filmed at Old Tucson Studios.

Old Tucson Studios offers a complete

Figure 22: The Grand Palace Hotel

western town with 75 buildings including 32 practical buildings. The 320-acre location sets within the Tucson Mountain Park in the Sonoran Desert. Although there are several areas around the studios that are allegedly haunted, one of the best known hauntings concerns the Grand Palace Hotel and Saloon.

The exterior of the Grand Palace Hotel and Saloon is a two story building with a balcony on three sides. The interior features a bar with a staircase capping the left side. Three mirrors are located behind the bar. The staircase leads up to an interior balcony and there are three unfinished hotel rooms. The balcony also features several opera boxes looking down onto a performance stage located at the front of the saloon.

Several ghosts, including one of a little girl, have been spotted throughout the building, usually by security guards. The little girl is often spotted on the stairs leading to the second floor. Adjoining the saloon is Rosa's Cafe. The apparition of a young woman has been seen moving about Rosa's Cafe and reports of unusual noises and moving objects are common place.

The most active location within the studios is the Arizona Theater, also called "The Story Teller's". This is a small underground theater that many believe is haunted by a malevolent spirit.

Although there are a few exceptions, the ghost of the Arizona Theater mainly makes it presence known to women. When women enter the theater alone and sit in the back row of the theater in the dark, they began to hear noises on the stage which resemble footsteps. The footsteps then "jump" down off the stage and move towards the women at the rear of the theater.

A number of the security guards have also experienced this phenomenon. Often the security guards go down into the air conditioned basement theater and sit at the back row in the dark. The only sources of light are the two exit signs above the entry ways. At first they hear the sound of footsteps walking across the stage. Shortly thereafter an unseen presence jumps off the stage and moves up towards the rear of the theater, blocking out the light from the exit signs. They then hear the sound of heavy breathing or sometimes whispering in close proximity[7].

Suddenly, the subtle light coming from the theater's exit lights are blocked as if someone is

---

[7] Related by a former security guard and confirmed by the research of the Southwest Ghost Hunters Association.

standing before them. This is following by either a tapping sound or heavy breathing. Usually the women turn on a flash light at this point, revealing that no one is there.

On occasion, the ghost makes its presence known to men. This has only happened to male security guards that the "ghost" doesn't like. They often end up quitting their jobs and the few that have not refuse to enter the theater alone.

The school house is another studio building that has unusual phenomena associated with it. Security guards hear the sound of children and the lights go on and off by themselves. The door also seems to unlock itself, much to the dismay of the security guards.

The hauntings are not limited to specific buildings however. The ghost of a cowboy has been seen and heard walking about the town's streets. Security guards have heard the sound of footsteps and spurs moving down the streets surrounding the saloon and town hall. One security guard actually saw the "cowboy" walk right past her and through the locked door of one of the studio's shops.

Another phenomenon that occurs through the studios is called "Shadow man" by employees. Basically this being appears like a dark human figure that seems to follow (or stalk) security guards and visitors. Other unusual activities that occur are the random turning on of building lights around the studios.

Pioneer International Hotel

Figure 23: Pioneer International Hotel

The Pioneer Building was once the Pioneer International Hotel is located at the corner of Stone and Pennington Streets. Tucson received national attention in 1970 for fire at the Pioneer International Hotel, in which 29 people died. The tragedy began to unfold around midnight on Dec. 20, 1970[8], during a Christmas party for employees of Hughes Aircraft Co. (now Raytheon). A fire broke out and claimed the lives of 29 people.

The landmark Downtown hotel was packed with guests visiting to shop or celebrate the holidays. Included in those present were many prominent citizens from Arizona and Sonora, Mexico.

At a party on the ground floor, bandleader Louis Leon and other musicians caught the faint smell of burning. They thought the wires to their sound equipment must be overheating. Then the catering manager approached with a terse message that he wanted the bandleader to "get them the hell out of here. The place is on fire."

Leon recalled recently that guests filed out in an orderly manner. The bandleader went outside to move his car and looked up. "You could see the flames coming out of the hotel windows," he said. "Boy, that was really a nightmare."

---

[8] Volante, Eric, *New Scientific Knowledge of How Fire Behaves is Raising Questions About Whether Tucson's 1970 Pioneer International Hotel Fire Stemmed from Arson; New Probe Is Sought for Hotel Fire that Killed 29.* The Arizona Daily Star, TucsonMcClatchy-Tribune Business News

Old photos, interviews with witnesses and newspaper accounts paint a black picture of that night. A few guests clambered down a fire-escape tower. But acrid smoke and withering heat -- fueled mainly by the synthetic carpet that covered the floors and lower walls of the hallways -- spread rapidly through the top eight floors of the 11-story building and trapped others. As firefighters raced to the hotel, they listened to radio reports of people leaping from windows near Alameda Street.

One woman clung to a pipe outside her window. Some guests threw mattresses out windows, then jumped, only to be crushed against the pavement. Up in Room 722, a mother and her five children perished.

On the ninth floor, a gray-haired woman leaned out of a window at the rear of the hotel. She yelled again and again to firefighters, "I'm still here! My God, I'm still here! Minutes later, she plunged to her death.

On the 10th floor, a 31-year-old attorney, Paul E. d'Hedouville, died from carbon-monoxide fumes in his windowless room.

Businessman Harold Steinfeld, who had owned the hotel since 1929, and his wife, Peggy, were in their penthouse suite on the 11th floor.

"My husband talked to them (by phone) that night," the Steinfelds' niece, Bettina Lyons, recalled last week. "They said everything was fine, not to worry, the fire would be put out. They had heard from the desk downstairs that if they needed to, they'd come and get them."

After rescuers battled their way to the penthouse, one announced by radio that they thought that they had found Mr. and Mrs. Steinfeld. When asked if they were OK, the response was negative.

The couple, overcome by smoke, and 26 other people died. Another woman died months later of her injuries, bringing the toll to 29.

The tragedy tore the hearts of families on both sides of the U.S.-Mexican border. A then-16-year-old hotel employee, Louis Cuen Taylor, was convicted of intentionally starting the fire and is serving a life sentence at the state prison in Florence.

The hotel "never recovered again. Even though they put money into it and put sprinkler systems in, people did not come to stay," Lyons said.

"And because the Pioneer Hotel was lost, all the people who came to shop Downtown did not come there. And one by one the stores began to die. So I would say it had an enormous effect on Downtown and the community. It probably changed it irreparably. And it's still struggling."

Rebuilt after a fire killed trapped occupants on the upper floors, it is said that the hotel is haunted by the spirits of those who died in the fire. Witnesses have reported hearing strange sounds, smelling smoke and seeing people trying to escape the flames.

People working in renovated Pioneer Building offices today say that when they are working late, they sometimes hear footsteps and music playing, as if the holiday party were still in progress. There have also been accounts of people smelling smoke when nothing is burning, and of a small girl looking for her mother who was one of the maids at the hotel who perished in the fire.

Radisson Hotel

Figure 24: Tucson Radisson

The Radisson Hotel on East Speedway in believed to be haunted by a woman that was murdered by her boyfriend when he found out she was cheating on him with another man in the hotel. Her ghosts roams the halls but can also be seen in the kitchen and the ballroom, where she can be heard crying and moaning loudly for help. Her restless spirit seems to not be able to find peace, and seems to make it hard for some guests to find peace as well

Sabino Canyon

Figure 25: Sabino Canyon

The scenery at Sabino Canyon beautiful and you can enjoy the walking trails and views at the Sabino Canyon State Park. The park is home to a lot of wildlife though, and care should be exercised when hiking and walking alone, especially after dark.

There are many stories that a particularly malevolent, angry mountain lion likes to stalk and follow hikers and campers until they reach the main paved road. The spirit is said to have very negative energy and seems to be very angry. Be very prepared, not only with your sunscreen, cameras and maps, but know how much time you have before sundown as well. The last thing you want is an evil spirit pursuing you through these dark desert pathways

Sam Levitz Furniture Store

Figure 26: Sam Levitz Store/Warehouse

Sam Levitz moved to Tucson in the early forties. In 1953 he opened the Sam Levitz Furniture Store and in 1955 he opened the world's first Direct-to-You Furniture Warehouse. People came from miles around to see what Sam Levitz had to offer. At one location on 36th Street, Levitz's offers more than furniture, it offers a ghost.

According to local legend, many years ago a workman was up on one of the racks and tragically lost his balance fell off of the rack. He did not survive the fall. Witnesses have seen the man wearing a black shirt and a black hat moving about the store as if he still thinks he is working. They've also have had a psychic come into the building and try to make the figure go away but the man will not leave. His appearance usually happens between 4 a.m. & 5 a.m.

Magma Copper Mine

Figure 27: Magma Copper Mine

The Magma Copper Mine in San Manuel was one of the largest underground copper mines in the world. However, as has happened to so many mines over the years, it was closed. Of course, the closing of the mine does not stop those who feel it is their home from continuing their work.

55 Miners died while working the Magma Copper Mine, so the chances of this place being haunted is pretty high. In fact, workers on the mine today claim to see strange lights floating through the cave.

One worker was working along with a co-worker, chatting away with him for over 30 minutes when the co-worker just disappeared.

But the main ghost here is known as "White Boots". The story says that a miner was working deep in the mine and there was a very nasty accident and his body was cut in two. His top half was retrieved but his lower body was never found.

Many miners have reported seeing "white boots" floating around the caves, maybe this ghost is looking for his lost legs.

The stories of the hauntings of this mine go back many years. There have long been stories told of mine workers reporting seeing lights and encountering workers that they knew were not assigned to their level. Another miner reported having miner come into his line and help him work his area for over 45 minutes only to find out later that there wasn't another worker assigned to work on his level that entire day.

A mineworker died in a cave in when this mine was first being built and it is said that the body could not be recovered due to the size of the cave in. Many believe that it is the spirit of this dead miner that tries to help his fellow miners.

San Xavier Del Bac Mission

Figure 28: San Xavier del Bac Mission

The San Xavier del Bac Mission is situated in the Santa Cruz Valley nine miles south of Tucson, Arizona. Framed in the warm browns of the surrounding hills and the violet shadows of more distant mountains, it rises, brilliantly white from the desert floor of dusty green mesquite and sage. The imposing dome and lofty towers, the rounded parapets and graceful spires etched against the vivid blue complete a skyline with a graceful enchantment.

From the earliest times, the Tohono O'odham settlement in which the Mission is located was called Bac, "place where the water appears," because the Santa Cruz River, which ran underground for some distance, reappears on the surface nearby.

The celebrated Jesuit missionary and explorer, Father Eusebio Francisco Kino, first visited Bac in 1692. Eight years later in 1700, Father Kino laid the foundations of the first church, some two miles north of the present site of the Mission. He named it San Xavier in honor of his chosen patron, St. Francis Xavier, the illustrious Jesuit "Apostle of the Indies."

The present church was built from 1783 - 1797 by the Franciscan Fathers Juan Bautista Velderrain and Juan Bautista Llorenz. Little is known about the actual labor of the construction of the church, who was the architect, who were the artisans, but many believe it was the Tohono O'odham who fulfilled these roles. Why the one tower was never completed is still a mystery, but hopefully one day this question will be answered.

San Xavier Mission is acclaimed by many to be the finest example of mission architecture in the United States. It is a graceful blend of Moorish, Byzantine and late Mexican Renaissance architecture, yet the blending is so complete it is hard to tell where one type begins and another ends.

Figure 29: San Xavier Del Bac Mission

It is said that on the outside of the mission in the artwork on either side of the main doors there is a snake and on the other side a mouse. If the snake catches the mouse the end of time is near. Several people in the area have heard whispers of his story come from a shadowy figure of a man outside the church. He has been seen pointing to each sector as the story is told. Also there has been sighting of an old Padre wondering throughout the church, usually dusk or dawn, the time when candles needed to be lit, or extinguished. The specter of a nun is seen leading five children to the chapel from an out building that was once used a schoolhouse. The schoolhouse burnt to the ground killing all inside. It is believed the nun was trying to get the children to safety.

Figure 30: St. Mary's Hospital

St. Mary's Hospital

St. Mary's Hospital is located at 1601 W. St. Mary's Road and is the only major hospital on Tucson's Westside. St. Mary's Hospital, the first hospital in Arizona territory, was established in 1880 by the Sisters of St. Joseph on the west side of Tucson. Over the years, a coalition of hospitals in southern Arizona, starting with St. Mary's and St. Joseph's Hospitals in Tucson, became the Carondelet Health Network. Morrison Custom Management became food service provider for the Network in 1992.

With a hospital as old as St. Mary's there are bound to be stories about ghosts and hauntings. The building is huge, as the hospital has expanded from its original 12 beds to over 400. There are a number of different experiences that have been related by staff and patients, such as people seeing someone walking into an elevator and then disappearing. There have also been stories about elevators opening into strange places, strange people riding on the elevators with staff, and a host of other things, but the majority of the stories revolve around a nun on the fourth floor.

One night, one of the nursing staff was looking down the 4 north hallway and saw a nun standing in the middle of the hall, pointing into a room. The staff member went to see what was going on, but when she got there, the nun had disappeared. In the room that she was pointing at, there was a female patient who was suicidal and was attempting to take her life. The nun was warning the staff.

It is, presumably, the same nun that walks with staff along the hallway going from the North Halls to the West Halls. Members of the staff have seen her reflection in the glass windows at night as she follows them as they walk in the halls.

Tucson High Magnet School

The Tucson High Magnet School is located

Figure 31: Tucson High Magnet School

at 400 North Second Avenue. Tucson High is the premier magnet school in Tucson, specializing in four program areas: Fine Arts, Science, Technology and Math[9]. According to the locals, one of the many classrooms in the vocational building has been condemned because of rumors of a student killing himself there. Witnesses swear that the student now haunts the room. Students and teachers have reported hearing loud taps on the door, cold spots, and eerie footsteps when no one is around.

Tucson Medical Center

Figure 32: Tucson Medical Center

The Tucson Medical Center is located at 5301 E. Grant Road. A former worker at Tucson Medical Center for a year experienced strange and unsettling occurrences. This old hospital that dates

---

[9] http://edweb.tusd.k12.az.us/thms/newsite/magnetprogram.htm.

back to the 1940's holds many secrets. Staff members claim that they saw an apparition of an older woman dressed all in black roaming the hall near unit 450. She would walk through the walls and doors of that hall.

Also in the same hallway a child would also be seen to run through the doors and walls. It was also reported that some staff members had seen a black cat running through the wall of this dept. during various work shifts. There were also many cold spots in various locations of the hospital. The female co-workers experienced their hair being pulled and heard whispers in their ears as well as other strange sounds. There is one particular office chair with wheels would roll by itself.

Ghosts have been reported in the Education Building at TMC. One ghost is said to be a well-respected nurse who died of an unknown disease. The nurse is known as "The Lady in White". "The Lady in White" is friendly; she greets people and opens doors for them. Another ghost is an older man who took care of the horses when this building was a horse stable. The old man was murdered, stabbed to death with a pitchfork, on this site. The ghost of the old man is known as "The Cold Spirit." "The Cold Spirit" seems to enjoy making people uncomfortable.

Vail High School

Figure 33: Vail High School

Vail High School is a small comprehensive high school serving students in grades 9 – 12 with a maximum enrollment of 210 students. Its unique location in the University of Arizona Science and Technology Park allows the school to capitalize on business relationships and connects students to their futures.

However, at the same time that the school looks toward the future, it must somehow deal with the specters of the past. There have been rumors of spirit visions being seen in the male restrooms of

Vail High School. Sinks turn off and on while toilets tend to flush constantly when no one else is within the room. Teachers have reported seeing an adult male in the restroom, who, when confronted, disappears without a word in a split second.

Velasco Pueblo

The building is located at 471-477 South Stone Pueblo, in Tucson's Old Pueblo Section of the city. In 1850, this adobe home started off with 3 main rooms and an entry hall. Other sections of the house were added onto this main house, all the way up through the 1880's. These grander rooms have 15 foot high ceilings, constructed with Ponderosa Pine and Douglas Fir. A major renovation of the home took place when its most famous owners, Carlos Velasco and wife Beatriz, moved into the house, in 1878. Carlos Velasco accomplished much in his life. He would be classified as a real achiever. He was a Sonora State Senator, a district judge, a general store operator, started a Spanish newspaper right in this house, in one of the south rooms, and started a fraternal insurance society in response to growing anti- Hispanic feelings in the community.

As the years past, the adobe house fell into disrepair, and even suffered a fire in one of the bedrooms. Thankfully, the Velasco Pueblo was rescued by 3 new owners, Brown, Dillon and Cobb, who took on the huge project to renovate this historic pueblo to its former glory. However, it wasn't long before the new owners found out that they had an unexpected resident watching their renovation efforts.

- While working near the dark, wall-blackened by fire, bedroom, located off the room that was used for the Spanish newspaper business, Brown looked up and saw an apparition of an upper torso of a Mexican man, sporting a mustache, who was looking at Brown. After looking at pictures, Brown positively identified this apparition as being Carlos Velasco.

- At least 3 other occurrences of Senior Velasco standing or lounging in various parts of the adobe have been reported by other witnesses.

The ghost of Velasco when he makes himself visible to the living, looks directly, and steadily in a calm manner at the startled people. He likes to see the work that is being done to his house, and isn't upset at all with the renovation. He also likes to reset the clocks and rearranges the furniture in ways that are considered odd by the new owners.

Bank of America

Figure 34: Bank of America Sign

The Bank of America building is located at 902 N. Stone Avenue. The ghost of a bearded man has been seen in the bank lobby. He appears to be about 25 years old and of average height. Unexplained footsteps on the stairs and self-slamming doors have been reported. The feeling of cold spots around the building and the fragrance of heavy perfume adds to the legend.

Davis Monthan Air Force Base

Figure 35: Entrance sign for Davis Monthan Air Force Base

Davis–Monthan Air Force Base (DM AFB) (IATA: DMA, ICAO: KDMA, FAA LID: DMA) is a United States Air Force base located within the city limits approximately 5 miles (8.0 km) south-southeast of downtown Tucson, Arizona. It was established in 1925 as Davis-Monthan Landing Field. The host unit for Davis–Monthan AFB is the 355th Fighter Wing (355 FW) assigned to Twelfth Air Force (12AF), part of Air Combat Command (ACC). The base is best known as the location of the Air Force Materiel Command's 309th Aerospace Maintenance and Regeneration Group (309 AMARG), the aircraft boneyard for all excess military and U.S. government aircraft and aerospace vehicles. The base was named in honor of World War I pilots Lieutenants Samuel H. Davis (1896–1921) and Oscar Monthan (1885–1924), both Tucson natives. Davis, who attended the University of Arizona prior to enlisting in the Army in 1917, died in a Florida aircraft accident in 1921. Monthan enlisted in the Army as a private in 1917, was commissioned as a ground officer in 1918, and later became a pilot; he was killed in the crash of a Martin bomber in Hawaii in 1924.

The ghost of a WWII pilot wanders around the mothballed aircraft. When he is there patrol lights and flashlights don't work. It's been said that the ghost takes a path right through security fences, crosses Kolb road and disappears.

SANTA RITA HOTEL

Figure 36: Santa Rite Hotel

The Santa Rita Hotel, which was demolished in 2009 was located at 88 E. Broadway. There were several ghosts reported at this location. One of the main ghosts here, said to have been a Texas rancher that is known as "Ferguson" came to Tucson in search of his cheating wife and her lover. He had discovered that the baby she was carrying was not his but the lovers.

He shot them both in the hotel, he then went to elevator shaft where he hung himself, while others say he hung himself in Room 822. Ferguson's apparition used to be seen a lot in the hotel, he was known for playing with the lights and anything else electrical.

Many of the ghosts here were children. One ghost was a little boy who, when running around the pool, slipped and drowned. Wet footprints around the pool area would appear out of nowhere, it's thought that there from the ghost of the young boy who drowned in the hotels pool.

Many of the guests have complained of noisy children playing on some of the upper floors, but when the staff has gone to investigate the noise they find no one. Then there is the mysterious light that comes on in the tower, at times, though no one ever turned one on. Sometimes the light is golden, sometimes it is green.

Over the years there have been so many creepy goings on that has resulted in the staff being scared petrified by the ghosts harassing them.

On many occasions the security guards of the hotel phoned the police to report a break in, as they heard loud footsteps and see lights going on upstairs, but no one was ever found there.

There is another spirits that is known for throwing stones in the hallway, and laughing at the guests as they walk by, as well as moving the guests' belongings in their rooms, and opening the doors.

BARRIO HISTORICO HOUSE

Barrio Historico House is located at 46 W Simpson St. A man appears inside the bedroom. A little girl wearing a red and white striped dress and brown shoes also appears. The girl has been described as being about seven or eight years old with light brown braided hair. The little girl, named "La Muchachita," is reported to open drawers and then move framed photographs from room to room.

CHARLES O. BROWN HOUSE

The Charles O. Brown House is located at 40 E. Broadway. "A specter is haunting Downtown's historical Brown House - the specter of Clara Brown, some say. Ghost rumor has it that a very real spirit loiters around the old building, causing the hair on the back of one's neck to stand up." (Clara Brown, Downtown's Very Own Ghost) People who have seen a woman in a long dress standing in the parking lot have speculated that it is the ghost of Clara Brown, wife of Charles O.

Brown, who lived in Tucson until her death in 1932 at age 86.

EL TIRADITO

Figure 37: Wishing Shrine

El Tiradito (Wishing Shrine) is located at 221 S. Main Ave. There have been many reports of ghosts being seen here over the years. One of the reported ghosts is a child named Pedro. Pedro was a 6-year-old boy who was murdered near the shrine.

Office Building of Attorney Louis W. Barassi

The Office Building of Attorney Louis W. Barassi is at 485 S. Main Ave. In 2003, this office was occupied by attorney Louis W. Barassi. The attorney and his staff claimed that the building was haunted based on unexplained happenings. A heavy briefcase was forcefully slammed to the floor without any obvious reason. An attorney was forcefully pushed against the wall by an invisible force. Items on Barassi's desk had been found scattered.

Fort Lowell Park

Residents of the neighborhood of Fort Lowell Park report wispy figures and doors unlocking on their own. Laughter has been heard when no one is around. A soldier is said to have haunted the area in 1900. Residents shot at this ghost soldier but the bullets passed right through him.

22nd Street Antique Mall

The 22nd Street Antiques Mall is located at 5302 E. 22nd Street. There are several hauntings at this place. Furniture moves on its own. A woman in a long dress floating above the floor has been seen, as well as the ghost of a little girl. The sound of an antique typewriter typing when no one is around has been heard and a rocking chair rocks when no one is near it.

GRANT ROAD GHOST

The Grant Road Ghost can be found at 3402 E. Grant Road. Now known as Tom's Used Furniture, previously this spot was the Tia Elena, a Mexican food restaurant. This ghost, that is said to have ties to this location, is a woman that appears as a dark, shadowy figure.

INDEX

1

1873 stock market crash, 16

2

22nd Street Antiques Mall, 127

A

Ancient Gods, 4
Angel of Death, 4
Arizona, 30, 92, 94, 100, 109, 113
   Apache Junction, 61
   Douglas, 95, 118
   San Manuel, 107
   Tombstone, 81, 83, 85
   Tucson, 68, 69, 79, 85, 89, 94, 99, 100, 106, 109, 113, 114, 115, 118
Arizona Organic Act, 13
Arizona State Museum South, 54, 55, 56
Arizona Territory, 12, 13
Arizona Theater, 96, 97

B

Bank of America, 9, 120
Barrio Historico House, 125
Battle of Glorietta Pass, 13
Battle of Picacho Pass, 13
Battle of the Bulls, 11, 12
Baylor, Lt. Colonel John, 12

Bear Down Gym, 47, 48, 52, 53, 54
Billy the Kid, 6
Bloom Elementary, 71
Bloom Elementary School, 70
Bonilla's Elementary School, 62
Bucket of Blood Saloon, 18

C

California, 82, 83
California Column, 13
Cap'n Crunch Cereal, 67
Carondelet Health Network, 113
Catalina High School, 63
Centennial Hall, 24, 25, 27
Collier Elementary School, 71
Colossal Cave, 59, 60
Colossal Cave Mountain Park, 59
Columbia Pictures, 93

D

Davis Bilingual School, 8, 72
Davis, President Jefferson, 12
Davis–Monthan Air Force Base, 121
Desert Hills Behavioral Treatment Center, 68
Desert View High School, 73
Desert View Ranch, 74
Dillinger, John, 89, 90

E

Earp, Virgil, 82
Earp, Wyatt, 81, 83, 84, 85
Ebber's Building, 21
Education Building at TMC (Tucson Medical Center), 69
El Paso Southwest Railroad Depot, 81
El Tiradito, 126
English Building, 38, 39
Evergreen Cemetery, 8, 52, 74, 75

F

Ford, Harrison, 93
Fort Lowell Park, 10, 127
Fort Tucson, 12
Fox Theater, 78
Fox Tucson Theatre, 76, 77, 78
Francis Owen Holaway Elementary School, 85
Fred G. Acosta Job Corp Center, 79, 80

G

Gadsden Purchase, 11
Garcia's Restaurant, 81
George, 64, 66, 67, 84
Gotham, 86
Grand Palace Hotel and Saloon, 96
Grant Road Ghost, 128

H

Herring Hall, 53
Hohokam, 55, 59, 60
Hohokam Indians, 59
Holliday, Doc, 84

Hollywood in the Desert. *See* Old Tucson Studios
Hooter's Restaurant, 86
Horn, Dr. Ambrose L., 14, 19, 23
Hotel Congress, 88, 90

K

Kino Community Hospital, 65

L

La Posta Quemada Ranch, 59
Legend of Carlos, 33
Li'l Abner Steakhouse, 66
Luz Academy of Tucson, 68

M

Magma Copper Mine, 107
Main Campus Auditorium, 25
Maldenado, Carlos, 33
Maricopa Residence Hall, 31
Marroney Theater, 36
Mexican Occidente state, 11
Modern Language Building, 7, 39, 40, 41
Mormon Battalion, 11

N

New Mexico Campaign, 13
New West Nightclub, 86

O

Office Building of Attorney Louis W. Barassi, 10, 126
Old Jail, 92
Old Main, 14, 16, 32, 33, 34, 35
Old Pueblo Section, 118
Old Tucson Studios, 92, 93, 94, 95

Omega Press, 3

P

Papago, 94
Paul, Bob, 84, 85
Pioneer International Hotel, 99, 100
Presidio San Augustine del Tucson, 26

R

Radisson Hotel, 104
Romance Languages Lab, 40

S

Sabino Canyon, 9, 105
Salmon, John 'Button' Byrd, 48, 49, 50, 51, 52
Sam Levitz Furniture Store, 106
San Elizario, Texas, 5
San Xavier del Bac Mission, 109
Santa Rita Hotel, 123
Sonora, 100, 118
St. Joseph's Hospital, 113
St. Mary's Hospital, 112
Stillwell, Frank, 81

T

Territorial University of Arizona. *See* University of Arizona
Texas

El Paso, 3, 4, 5
The Bells of St. Mary's, 94
The Lady in White, 69
Tohono O'odham, 94
Tucson Cotillion Dance, 21
Tucson High Magnet School, 114
Tucson Livery Service, 15
Tucson Medical Center, 69, 115
Tucson Mountain Park, 96
Tucson train station, 82

U

Unidentified Flying Objects, 6
University Medical Center. *See* Kino Community Hospital
University of Arizona, 13, 14, 16, 17, 19, 21, 23, 24, 25, 29, 30, 32, 38, 39, 43, 47, 48, 52, 55, 57, 117, 122
University of Arizona Science and Technology Park, 117

V

Vail High School, 117
Velasco Pueblo, 119

W

Wang. Connie, 4
Wayne, John, 93
Woman's Athletic Field, 39

www.ingramcontent.com/pod-product-compliance
Lightning Source LLC
Chambersburg PA
CBHW071518080526
44588CB00011B/1479